RED LETTER DAY

Kestrel Kites is a series of lively and interesting stories intended for beginner readers. Clear, large print and lots of line drawings make these books ideal for those who have just begun to enjoy reading a complete book on their own.

ALEXA ROMANES

RED LETTER DAY

ILLUSTRATED BY KRYSTYNA TURSKA

A Kestrel Kite · VIKING KESTREL

For Broughton County
Primary School

VIKING KESTREL

Penguin Books Ltd, Harmondsworth, Middlesex, England
Viking Penguin Inc., 40 West 23rd Street, New York, New York 10010, U.S.A.
Penguin Books Australia Ltd, Ringwood, Victoria, Australia
Penguin Books Canada Limited, 2801 John Street, Markham, Ontario, Canada L3R 1B4
Penguin Books (N.Z.) Ltd, 182–190 Wairau Road, Auckland 10, New Zealand

First published 1986
Text copyright © Alexa Romanes, 1986
Illustrations copyright © Krystyna Turska, 1986

British Library Cataloguing in Publication Data

Romanes, Alexa
   Red letter day. – (Kestrel kites)
   I. Title
   823'.914[J]   PZ7

   ISBN 0–670–81086–X

Printed in Great Britain by
Richard Clay (The Chaucer Press) Ltd,
Bungay, Suffolk
Set in 16/22pt Palatino

Chapter One

It was a warm, sleepy afternoon at Rockdown Primary School. The heating was still on although spring sunshine streamed through the windows. In the Class Three hut, the infants leaned against each other drowsily as Mrs Padfield read them a story. In the main building, the twenty first and second year juniors drooped over their topic books, their pencils barely creeping across the pages. The top class, next door, yawned one after the other as the headmaster hunted for a piece of chalk.

In his desk drawer, overflowing with old biros, string, drawing pins, recorder cleaners and Banger Morgan's Action Man (confiscated for being used as an offensive

weapon in the playground), Mr Fisher
found a stub of white chalk. He turned to
the board and wrote rapidly in capitals

A RED LETTER DAY

With a tap and squeak of chalk he added
an exclamation mark, spun round to face the
class and said in a Wake Up At The Back
voice, 'A Red Letter Day! Who can tell me
what that is?'

Clare Wilkins's hand shot up, but the rest
of the class were too sleepy to give their
usual groan at her eagerness.

'Sir! I know Sir!' she announced proudly.

Clare Wilkins had only just moved up from Class Two and was anxious to make an impression. 'It's an important day. A special day.' Mr Fisher beamed at her.

'Quite right, Clare.' He looked round the rest of the class without much hope. 'I don't suppose anyone knows *why* special days are called Red Letter Days?' There was a heavy silence, except for what might have been a faint snore from Banger Morgan. His head was very low over his desk. Even Clare did not answer.

The head sighed and explained about saints' days and holidays being marked in red on old-fashioned calendars. He spoke quietly for a while, and then played one of his favourite tricks, which was suddenly to turn up the volume.

'RIGHT CLASS ONE – ON THE DOUBLE! A LIST OF IMPORTANT DAYS . . . PATRICK EAST BEGIN!'

Eggy East stopped in mid-yawn. (Eggy, because East becomes Easter which becomes Egg.) He tried to straighten his face and open his eyes. His brain, which had been on automatic pilot, switched on again.

'Christmas!' he offered triumphantly.

'Good.' The head's chalk skimmed across the top of the board. There was a lot of space left. 'Tom Morgan?'

Kindly, Eggy East gave his friend a dig in the ribs. Banger (the butcher's son) Morgan awoke with a snort.

'Think of a special day,' hissed Eggy.

'Friday?' tried Banger.

'Why is Friday a special day?' asked Mr Fisher. There was an expectant hush.

''Cos we have sausages for tea,' replied Banger with a blissful smile. The class roared with laughter. Taking advantage of them all being awake, Mr Fisher pounced on the next child. The list began to grow.

Soon it read

Christmas
My Birthday
Cup Final Day
When Auntie Takes Me Out
The School Trip
When the Fair Comes
The Village Disco
Harvest Festival
The Small Schools Choir Competition
Sports Day
When My Brother Has a Bath
The Fête and Flower Show

The blackboard was now covered. Mr
Fisher drew a line under the last
suggestion.

'The Fête and Flower Show,' he reminded
the class, 'is the next Red Letter Day in the
village.' A buzz of noise went round the
class. It would be in eight weeks' time,

towards the end of June. The head went on,
'The school, of course, will be making its
usual contributions with the maypole
dancing, the tombola, and the Princess who
will be the attendant for the Rockdown
Queen.' (The buzz grew louder among the
girls.) 'After break I shall put all the Class
One girls' names, as usual, into a hat for the
choosing of the Princess. Maypole practice

with Miss Gale begins on Monday. Gifts for the tombola can be brought to school from now on.' (There were sighs from some of the class, knowing the reception this message would get at home.) 'In the meantime, I want a page of writing about any of the Red Letter Days we have listed.' Mr Fisher looked at the board again and rubbed out 'When My Brother Has a Bath'.

'Choose another subject, Patrick East.' Eggy's brother had left the school only last year. Mr Fisher did not wish to be reminded of him.

All through afternoon break, girls stood in excited groups discussing who might be chosen as Princess.

'It's great to be the Princess,' sighed Clare Wilkins. 'You get a beautiful long dress made specially for you, and a sash with "Rockdown Princess" on it in gold

11

letters. And you get a bouquet, and money to spend on all the Fête sideshows — and your photograph taken for the newspapers!'

There were five girls in the fourth year and six in the third year, and the only one of them not desperate to be this year's Princess was Bonnie Dean.

'I hope I don't get picked,' she said. The others looked at her in disbelief. 'You have to sit with the Queen on a decorated float and go through the village with everybody staring at you. Anyway, the Princess can't do the maypole dancing. I'd much rather do that.'

After break, the headmaster came into the classroom carrying a peculiar velvet hat left over from last week's jumble sale. There was, for Class One, an unusual silence. The vicar, who always helped to run the Fête, came in too. He talked about the event for a while, but Clare Wilkins wasn't listening.

She had her eyes shut tight and was chanting to herself, inside her head, 'Oh, *please* let me be Princess, *please* let me!' She was concentrating so hard that she only just opened her eyes in time to see the vicar dip his hand into the hat. The clock on the wall above his head ticked importantly, the gerbils scrabbled around their cage, and next door, Miss Gale's class were giving their unique version of the Banana Boat Song, loudly, cheerfully, out of tune – and heavy on the percussion. Rockdown School was as quiet as it could be, and Class One held its breath.

Chapter Two

'Bonnie Dean,' said the vicar solemnly, as if he were announcing a hymn. Bonnie made a small sound like a strangled hiccup. Clare took a deep breath and ground her teeth. Most of the boys cheered. They liked Bonnie because she was always willing to make up the numbers for football. (It's very difficult to make up complete teams in a small school.) The vicar tipped the bits of paper into the wastepaper basket and Mr Fisher began to hand out some books for the last lesson. It was over.

Clare was furious. She would have made a much better Princess than Bonnie. Her hair was long and fair ('just like a fairy-tale princess' her mum always said) and she would have looked just right. Bonnie would be all wrong, tall and awkward with her mousy hair and glasses. Whoever heard of a Princess with glasses! Even one of the Barker twins would have been better, brace and all. She could have kept her mouth shut and it wouldn't have shown.

Bonnie's mood was not much better than Clare's as she walked home at three-thirty. She had always enjoyed the Fête day before, and now it was something to be dreaded instead of looked forward to. Gloomily, she pushed open the gate of her next-door neighbour's garden. She always came to Mrs Lock's after school because her mother didn't get back from work until half-past five. The worst thing would be telling her mother that she was to be Princess. There's nothing more awful than your mother being thrilled about something you think is the absolute pits.

Meanwhile, Eggy and Banger had been cornered in the cloakroom by Miss Gale. Miss Gale was tall, with red hair and fierce blue eyes. It was difficult to avoid Miss Gale when she wanted to Have Words.

'I want a word with you, Patrick and Tom. What's this I hear from Mr Fisher about you not wanting to do maypole

dancing this year?' Eggy and Banger shuffled about uneasily. They had agreed between them that they were far too old now for that sort of thing, but they had reckoned on having the whole weekend to think of an excuse for Miss Gale.

'We can't do it this year,' muttered Eggy, playing for time. Banger looked longingly at the door.

'Why not?' demanded Miss Gale.

'Er . . . um . . . *you* tell Miss Gale why, Banger.' Banger's jaw dropped. It wasn't fair! It had been Eggy's idea to get out of the maypole dancing.

'No, *you* tell her,' he said coldly, collecting his sweater from his peg.

'Well, er, Banger and me thought we would sort of concentrate on the Pairs Fancy Dress this year . . .' invented Eggy.

'You can do both, surely?' Miss Gale had put on her patient voice. 'The fancy dress parade comes first and the maypole dancing later on in the afternoon.'

'But the idea we've got is very complicated. There wouldn't be time to change.' Both boys were edging towards the door.

'Oh, all right.' Miss Gale gave up. 'I suppose we can just about manage without you . . .' The door to the playground crashed shut again. Eggy and Banger had gone.

Clare and her younger brother, Gary, walked home across the allotments. They were squabbling over a booklet that Gary was holding behind his back.

'Oh, go on, Gary,' said Clare, impatiently. 'Let's have a look.'

'No.' Gary's round face was pink and determined. 'I got mine from the shop. You go and get your own.'

18

'I'm not going all the way back to the
High Street just for a measly Show
programme. So let me have a look at what
the children's classes are this year – or I'll
tell Mum who it was broke the hook off the
bathroom door.'

Gary was used to his sister's threats. She
meant it. He threw the booklet at her and
marched on ahead between the neat rows
of pea-sticks and bean-poles. Clare pounced
on it, smoothed it out and turned to the
back page, reading it quickly. Then she ran

to catch up with her brother.

'Are you entering something?' This was a pointless question. Everyone knew Gary loved entering things, from the Kiddies' Puzzle Corner in the local paper, to the talent contest at the school Christmas party.

'Miniature garden, eight to elevens, animal made from a vegetable, eight to elevens, a picture of what Rockdown might have looked like a hundred years ago, eight to elevens, and sponge cake – open to all,' he rattled off, without looking at the programme.

Clare was not impressed.

'You won't win any of *those*! Specially the open class. You're only eight and all the Women's Institute will enter that one.' Gary was not dismayed. He had been making cakes ever since he was big enough to stir a spoon, and he could make a better sponge cake than his mum could.

'What are you entering, then?' he asked his sister, calmly.

'Don't think I'll bother.' Clare swung her Mickey Mouse lunch-box casually. 'Tell you what I will win this year – Miss Gale's prize for the best maypole dancer. It'll be just as much my Red Letter Day as Bonnie Dean's, Princess or no. You wait and see!'

'We've got to enter the Fancy Dress at the Fête, now that you've told Miss Gale,' Banger grumbled to Eggy.

'So?' Eggy grinned. 'It beats prancing around the flipping maypole! We'll enter the pairs section, so we can do something together.'

Banger sighed heavily. 'You realize we'll have to do it all ourselves? My mum's about to have a baby, and you're always saying your mum can't sew for toffee.'

'We'll think of something that doesn't need sewing,' promised Eggy. They were walking along the lane to Eggy's house, and just then a long, red estate car swished past them and turned into a drive ahead.

'There go those kids from Bridge House,' said Eggy. 'They always enter the Pairs Fancy Dress.'

'And they always win!' pointed out Banger.

'Well, this year, just for once, they aren't going to. We are. So get thinking, Banger. We've got to come up with a really fantastic idea!'

Chapter Three

On Monday morning, Clare found a red crayon and filled in the figure 26 on the June part of the calendar on the kitchen wall. Gary was puzzled. He had not had Mr Fisher's talk about special days.

'I'm turning the Fête into a Red Letter Day,' Clare told him. 'It's going to be an extra special day this year, because the Fête has been going in the village for a hundred years. The vicar told our class.'

Miss Gale reminded the dancers of this fact before they began the maypole practice after school. The display had to be particularly good this year and they would be taking notes home about the clothes they were to wear. The idea was for them

to look like children did a hundred years
ago. There were murmurs of interest from
the girls and suspicion from the boys, but
Miss Gale was not one to allow much time
for gossip. With the help of Mr Fisher and
the caretaker, the maypole had been
brought out of its storage place in the scout
hut. Eager volunteers from Class One had
rediscovered the socket in the middle of the

grass behind the kitchen. They cleared it of earth, stones and woodlice, and now crowded round the maypole as it lay on the ground, its brightly coloured ribbons tied to its sides with string.

'Everyone stand well back,' roared Mr Fisher. 'We don't want an accident at the first practice.'

The pole was a seven-metre-long tube

with a metal core at the bottom for sinking into the hole in the ground. At the top were two metal discs, a large one over a smaller one. Each disc had eight ribbons fastened to it, making an inner and an outer circle for sixteen dancers.

The ribbons, as Miss Gale always called them, weren't made of ribbon at all, but were the same material as the bands the children wore when playing team games. Clare got quite excited as she watched the teachers and the caretaker struggle to raise the pole into the right position for slipping into the socket. She would have an outer ribbon again this year. The inners didn't have such complicated things to do, so they would be mainly Class Three. She hoped she would have a red ribbon this year. At the moment, red was her lucky colour.

As usual, the first practice was chaos. There were infants and new children who

had never done it before, the tape recorder wasn't working properly and there was a high wind. The little ones kept letting go of the ribbons and the wind whipped them high above their heads, tangling them with the other ribbons.

'Rule number one,' panted Miss Gale, leaping to retrieve them. '*Never* let go of your ribbon!' Clare hung on to hers tightly and grinned as Carlene Barker put up both hands to rescue a hair slide and her ribbon went flying.

Not much dancing got done that afternoon. The children practised handling the ribbons, learning how to make them longer or shorter as they wove in and out. Miss Gale sorted out who was doing which dance. Clare was pleased. She was doing four out of the five dances in the display, including her favourite, the Spider's Web. She felt she had a good chance of winning

Miss Gale's prize if she worked hard at it. The only other Class One person who might have been in the running was Bonnie Dean, and she was out of it. The Princess had to sit with the Queen all the time and couldn't dance.

Bonnie's mother had collected her in the car after school, having got away from work early. They were driving into town to look for a pattern and material for Bonnie's Princess dress. Bonnie tried to take an interest, but she was thinking about the maypole practice going on without her. As a fourth year, she could have helped the new ones.

She would miss the dancing. She didn't mind being looked at if she was doing something with a crowd of others, like in the display. But to sit on a platform with Linda Foster, the Queen, to be stared at . . .

that was a different matter. She rubbed at
her glasses with her cuff and concentrated
on the book of patterns her mother was
showing her. It was crowded in the store,
it was getting late and Mrs Dean was
becoming impatient.

'You must make up your mind, Bonnie.
We've the material and trimmings to find
yet, and the store closes soon.'

Bonnie looked at the pages covered

with pictures of bridesmaid-type dresses.
None of the girls in the drawings was a bit
like her, so it was difficult to imagine how
she would look. Eventually she pointed to
one that looked fairly plain, with a high
waist and puffed sleeves. Mrs Dean bought
the pattern and whisked Bonnie around the
rolls of materials until they found
something they both liked. The effect was
pale green, but the material was patterned

with tiny flowers and leaves. Bonnie
approved. She had been afraid she would
have to wear a bright, shiny dress with lots
of frills. It would be bad enough being
draped with the sash that said PRINCESS
in big silver letters.

Eggy and Banger lay on the grass in
Eggy's back garden, looking at the sky and
trying to have a brilliant idea before tea.
Banger's house, which was joined to the
butcher's shop next door, didn't have a
garden, only a yard with the cold store and
a space for the van to turn round. Eggy's
garden made up for that by being full of
long grass, old fruit bushes and trees that
were good for climbing.

Scuff, Banger's dog, was with them. He
was a big, ugly mongrel with bold, bright
eyes, a shaggy coat and an enormous
appetite. As well as bones and scraps from

the butcher's shop, he ate bread, cheese, cakes, fruit, the cat's dinner – in fact anything left within his reach. He sprawled beside the boys, cocking his head at each of them in turn as they spoke.

'Robin Hood and the Sheriff of Nottingham.'

'Mm . . . maybe . . . Tom and Jerry?'

'Someone did that last year.'

'What about paratroopers? We've got all the gear.'

'Too easy. We'd never beat the Bridge House kids with that. Was it last year they came as Worzel Gummidge and Aunt Sally?'

'The year before. Last year was Queen Elizabeth the First and Sir Francis Drake. Fantastic costumes they were.'

'Hired them, betcha!' Eggy rolled on to his stomach and pulled up handfuls of grass. 'We've got to think of something clever, but not so clever that people can't tell straight away what we are. And it mustn't cost anything, 'cos I'm nearly broke.'

'Me too . . . I can't think of any more ideas. Perhaps after tea. I'm too hungry to think.' Just then his father called from the kitchen, so Banger and Scuff took the short cut up a pile of old bricks and over the fence.

'Banger!' called Eggy. He skidded to a halt in the yard. Eggy looked at him seriously from the other side of the fence. 'I could go as an egg, and you could be a sausage.'

Banger thought for a moment and then said, equally seriously, 'Too dangerous. We might get eaten.' Eggy threw a handful of grass at him and then went indoors for his own tea.

It was nearly bedtime, while he was skimming through a comic, when Eggy had the brainwave.

'Got it!' He stuffed the comic into his school bag. 'Just wait till I tell Banger this one!'

Chapter Four

Mr Fisher decided to turn the Rockdown Fête into a project for the whole school. Each child made a folder in which they had to write their plans for June the 26th. Afterwards they would have to make a report on the day itself. This was all very well for the maypole dancers or the girls in the Rockdown Majorettes, but the would-be competitors for the Fancy Dress and the Show classes were worried.

'Sir,' complained Eggy, for all of them, 'we have to keep our ideas secret, in case someone else pinches them.'

'That's all right, Patrick,' the head told him. 'I shall collect all the folders in at the end of the lesson and keep them in a safe place.' Even so, Eggy and Banger were careful to discuss their ideas in whispers and to write with their free arms curved protectively round their paper.

At break they found a quiet spot in the playground to continue making plans. When Eggy had shown his friend the copy of *Horror Fun* first thing that morning, Banger had recognized it at once as the perfect idea.

'Frankenstein's Monster and the Mummy from the Tomb! That's brill, Eggy!' The idea appealed to their ghoulish imaginations, but now they had to work out how to do it.

'I've had a good idea already,' began Eggy excitedly, as they slid out of sight behind the infants' classroom. 'I can make myself taller with a false bit on top of my head and stilts, and I'll get rubber gloves to make horrible hands, and I've worked out a way of making a bolt through my neck and . . .'

'Hang on . . .' interrupted Banger. '*You're* being the Monster and *I'm* being the Mummy?'

'Well, yes.'

Banger thought for a moment. In theory, the Mummy ought to be a lot less work.

'Where will I get bandages from?' he wanted to know.

'Torn-up sheets,' suggested Eggy, instantly. Banger shook his head.

'Not from my mum. Remember the Roman togas for the school play?' He had paid the penalty for raiding the airing cupboard in his mother's absence.

'I could get you some strips of curtain lining,' said an interested voice behind them. The boys spun round. Bonnie Dean was leaning against the wall. She must have heard every word. 'Mum's been making lots

of curtains for people. I could get you
masses of strips. You'd only have to join
them up.'

The boys looked at each other and
nodded. Bonnie was O.K.

'Get as much as you can, then,' ordered
Eggy. 'And don't forget – this is a deadly
secret. We want to give everyone a good
scare.'

'Course I won't tell anyone,' promised Bonnie. 'I only wish I could be a monster too, instead of stuck up on the float looking like a piece of left-over wedding cake!' She started to leave them and then turned back. 'Tell you what, Banger, you ought to enter Scuff with you. He'd make a great werewolf.' The boys looked at each other again and wide smiles spread across their faces. Bonnie was a genius!

As the week of the Fête drew nearer, practices and preparations increased. Eggy and Banger were so full of themselves that everyone knew something was up. Gary, who had always looked on the pair as heroes, shadowed them everywhere, begging to be let in on the secret, but the boys were firm. If Gary knew, Clare would have it out of him in five minutes, and Clare was a blabbermouth. Defeated, Gary got on with his own preparations for the show. He painted his picture of the village a hundred years ago and put it between two big books to keep it flat and smooth. He begged a large dinner plate from his mother and started to collect moss and gravel and other bits and pieces for the miniature garden. He poked around the boxes in the village shop looking for unusual shaped vegetables to make his animal, and gave his mother a list of ingredients needed for his cooking.

'Goodness, Gary, you are organized this year,' she commented. Gary nodded. His rotten sister could jeer all she liked. The school was going to do a big wall display in the hall after the show, and he was making sure there would be some red first prize cards with the name Gary Wilkins on up there.

Clare pretended not to notice her

younger brother's preparations. As far as she was concerned, the highlight of the day would be the maypole dancing, with sixteen dancers making perfect patterns in the sunshine. Only one dancer would be a little more perfect than all the rest . . .

The last practice on the Friday before the great day went really well. The couple who always played the accordion and the fiddle arrived, so they were able to do it with the proper music. They were all trying out their new costumes – knee breeches, shirts and caps for the boys, white pinafores over flowered dresses for the girls. The only thing Clare didn't like were the black tights, which Miss Gale said 'looked very Victorian'.

'Of course,' Miss Gale added, 'you should all have buttoned boots, but we couldn't manage that. Anyway, black plimsolls are much safer.'

Clare was glad they had escaped the boots. It was going to be hot enough, if today was anything to go by. Tomorrow all the girls would have circlets of flowers in their hair. She hoped they wouldn't wilt.

On her way home, Bonnie was also thinking about what she would be wearing next day. She walked quickly, however, knowing her mother had the day off work and would be at home. To her surprise, she could hear the sewing machine whirring busily as she came through the door. Her Princess dress had been finished ages ago. What could her mother be doing? She ran into the back room to find her mother sitting in front of the machine surrounded by heaps of red and white silky material and festoons of rich-looking gold braid. Sequins and imitation jewels littered the table. Bonnie stared.

'What on earth is all this for, Mum?'

Mrs Dean groaned. 'Oh, Mrs Bell at Bridge House rang me in a panic. Her dressmaker has gone down with summer 'flu and hasn't finished the children's costumes for the Fancy Dress tomorrow. It's the King and Queen of Hearts. Isn't it gorgeous?' Bonnie nodded, half-heartedly. 'Do you mind getting your own tea, love? I've got to keep going with this to have any hope of finishing this evening.'

Bonnie nodded again. But she wasn't thinking about tea. She was feeling very sorry for Eggy and Banger and their hopes of beating the Bridge House kids. Even with Scuff the Werewolf, she didn't think they stood a chance.

Chapter Five

The weather forecast was right. This particular Saturday was going to be a scorcher. Gary got up early to put the finishing touches to his Show entries. He had stuck his picture on to a bigger piece of black paper to give it a frame, and it looked quite good. The sponge cake had risen perfectly and sparkled with a light dusting of sugar.

He checked his spider. Its green pepper body gleamed, its eight runner-bean legs were fastened securely and its baby tomato eyes were joined to the body with long pins. Very effective! He turned his attention to the miniature garden he had made the night before. On one side was a mossy rockery of tiny stones and little sprigs of heather. A silver paper stream ran down into a pool made with a mirror from an old powder compact. A minute duck, lent reluctantly by Clare, floated on the pool. A sandy path wound round beds of the tiniest flower heads he could find, leading to a hedge with a little gate made of matchsticks. Not bad at all. The trickiest part would be getting the garden and the other things safely to the Show tent. Luckily Dad had offered to run him down in the car.

Bonnie and her mother had a very early lunch and got down to the serious business of getting dressed. Clean white socks, clean nearly-new sandals, long white petticoat. Then the dress, lifted carefully over her head, hooks and eyes up the back. Her mother smoothed down the skirt and they

46

looked in the mirror.

'Very nice,' purred Mrs Dean. Bonnie couldn't tell. She had taken off her glasses to put on her dress. She reached for them. 'You're going to leave your glasses off for the afternoon, aren't you, dear?'

Bonnie looked at her mother with fond exasperation. Really, she could be so silly sometimes.

'Of course not! It's bad enough having to sit around all afternoon without not being able to see what's going on.'

'But Bonnie,' began her mother. There might have been a row, but they were interrupted by a knock at the door. It was the vicar's wife. She had brought flowers on two little combs for Bonnie's hair and a posy for her to carry. Mrs Dean forgot about the glasses in the excitement of admiring the flowers.

Clare looked out of her bedroom window as she brushed her long blonde hair. She could see into Miss Gale's garden from here. The head of the maypole was lying on the grass near the door, without the ribbons. The pole itself had been taken to the Show ground behind the village hall, and Miss Gale was probably giving the ribbons a last-minute iron, like she usually did. The maypole would be raised just before the procession of the Queen's float, the Majorettes and the fancy dress contestants arrived. The judging of the fancy dress would take place beforehand, at two o'clock on the green by the church.

Clare fixed a circle of flowers on her head and smiled at herself in the mirror. She was glad she wasn't entering anything this year. It meant that she could concentrate hard on one thing – winning Miss Gale's best dancer prize.

She glanced out of the window again. Miss Gale ought to get a move on. It was a quarter to two already. A lorry full of scrap metal and other junk had drawn up outside Miss Gale's house. Two men climbed out and knocked at the door. Clare

watched as a harassed-looking Miss Gale
appeared, waved a hand to the side of the
garden nearest to Clare's house, and
disappeared indoors again. The men picked

up an old bicycle and some pieces of corrugated iron. Then, Clare saw one of the men scoop up the head of the maypole and throw it on to the back of the lorry as well.

She stood rooted to the spot with her mouth open for five seconds while the full horror of the situation sank in. Then she flung herself down the stairs and out of the house just in time to see the lorry roar off down the street. This time she didn't hesitate. It was time for action. Clare began to run.

In the bedroom over the Morgans' shop, Banger and Eggy were still working on their disguises. Eggy was nearly finished. The papier-mâché forehead, with tufts of horse-hair sprouting from the scalp, bolts sticking out above huge ears and a scarred, bulging forehead, was firmly fixed under his chin with elastic. More horse-hair (pulled out secretly from underneath the old sofa) made shaggy eyebrows. He had stuck bits of burst pink balloon to his cheeks and under his chin, to look like saggy, wrinkled skin. In between he had glued plasticine warts. Thanks to a swift raid on his mother's make-up drawer, he also had blue lips, red-rimmed eyes and blacked-out teeth. He wore an old torn shirt of his father's and a pair of trousers, far too long in the leg, rolled up for the time being. He had yet to put on his paint-can stilts and his rubber-glove hands because he had to help Banger with his bandages.

Bonnie had given them four carrier bags of white cotton strips. 'It's like trying to untangle giant spaghetti,' complained Banger as they sorted them out. Between them they managed to wrap his legs, arms and body, but Banger's head proved difficult.

'Let's colour your face green,' suggested Eggy. 'Then we could leave useful bits showing – like your eyes and mouth.'

'And my nose.' Banger was anxious. 'I want to be able to breathe!'

Eventually the bandaging was finished, to Banger's relief, and Eggy began to apply artistic trickles of green slime. For some strange reason, Scuff found the slime attractive and tried to lick it off. The mongrel himself looked magnificent. His long coat had been soaked in starch and water, then dried out in spikes. Banger had made him a cardboard collar bristling with silver-foil points.

'We'll have to skip the red blood stuff we were going to put round his jaws,' said Eggy, regretfully. 'He'd probably love that too and slurp it off. I think he looks awful enough, anyway.' Muffled grunts of agreement came from Banger.

Eggy reached for some plastic bags filled with white powder and carefully poked holes in them with a needle. The scent of Mrs East's lily-of-the-valley talcum powder filled the room. Eggy chuckled as he attached the bags to Banger's back.

'Crumbling mummy dust!' he gloated. 'This'll finish off the judges – this and my bloody hands!' He pulled on the carefully prepared gloves. The raspberry juice in the fingers felt suitably disgusting and should drip out of the pin holes when he swung his hands. He looked at the clock. Five

minutes to get to the church. Just right. He picked up the paint tins.

'Come on, Banger. Take care Scuff doesn't trip you over.'

Frankenstein's Monster, the Mummy from the Tomb and the Werewolf of Rockdown thundered down the stairs, through the kitchen and out of the back door.

Mr and Mrs Morgan, who were enjoying a quiet cup of tea before going to the Fête, looked at one another with amazement.

'What on earth was that?' demanded Mr Morgan.

'Just Tom and Patrick and the dog,' quavered Mrs Morgan, pouring herself another strong cup, '. . . I *think*.'

The boys had planned their arrival for the judging of the Fancy Dress. They would appear at the last possible moment, by way of the churchyard, to create the best effect. First, however, Eggy had to put on his stilts. He had already made holes in the top of the cans either side of where his feet would go and had threaded them with

string. The boys stopped outside the shop
and Eggy stood on the cans, tying up the
string as tight as he could and rolling down
his trousers.

'Fantastic!' cried the Mummy, spitting
green slime.

'Keep your mouth closed till we get
there,' advised the Monster. 'And put Scuff
on the lead. We don't want to lose him.'

Scuff never went for walks without sloping off to the nearest dustbin or kitchen door, so Banger fastened the lead to the spiky collar. Lurching and clanking, Eggy led the way up the street.

They were passing Miss Gale's house just as she came running round from the side of the house. She was wearing a long skirt, a

high-necked old-fashioned blouse and a straw hat trimmed with flowers. The boys were puzzled by this get-up, until they remembered about the dancers being Victorian this year. Miss Gale looked anxiously up and down the road and then stared incredulously at Eggy, Banger and Scuff.

'Who are you?' She took a nervous step backwards.

'Only Eggy and Banger,' apologized the Monster.

'Good grief! . . . Look, has either of you seen a lorry full of rubbish?' Miss Gale sounded almost tearful, and her face was pink.

'No, miss,' chorused the boys.

'Something dreadful has happened. I've lost the top of the maypole!' Lost it? The efficient Miss Gale? The boys couldn't believe it until it was explained.

'I don't know what to do,' finished Miss

Gale, leaning against the garden wall. Scuff
gave a sympathetic whine. 'I should be up
at the green now, with the dancers. How
can I tell them that there won't be anything
for them to dance round?'

Clare caught up with the lorry at the
dead-end of Weaver's Lane, where the men

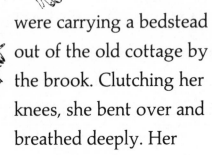

were carrying a bedstead
out of the old cottage by
the brook. Clutching her
knees, she bent over and
breathed deeply. Her
white shoes were covered in dust and the
flowers were sliding over one eye. When

she had recovered from the stitch in her
side, she gasped, 'The top of our maypole
. . . it's in your lorry!' But her voice came
out in a puffing squeak and the men
ignored her.

'Out of the way, love, we're in a hurry.'

'Wait . . . wait!' Clare pleaded, but the
men were already climbing into the cab of
the lorry and the engine was starting up. A
hot fury began to creep over Clare. They
were *not* going to get away with it. They
were *not* going to ruin her lovely Red
Letter Day by taking away the vital part of

the maypole. As the lorry began to move,
she ran to the back of it, found a foothold
and put her arms up to hang on to the
tailboard.

As the lorry emerged from Weaver's
Lane back into the High Street, it was
spotted by Miss Gale.

'That's it!' she shrieked. 'Quick! We must
catch it up!' Eggy began to clank after her.

'Eggy!' Banger called despairingly. 'What

62

about the judging?' Just then he heard the
church clock striking two in the distance.
He shrugged and began to run.
Immediately, Scuff, barking excitedly, swung
in front of him, nearly knocking him over.
Drat, the bandages were slipping over his
eyes. Quickly, Banger tied the Werewolf's
lead to Miss Gale's gate and lumbered off
after the others.

Gary was in a fever of excitement. Had
he won any prizes in the Show? The judges
would have finished making their decisions
by now. The flowers, vegetables, crafts and
children's entries would all be waiting to be
seen, with the coloured prize cards scattered
among them. But the Show tent did not
open until three o'clock, after the crowning
of the Queen and the dancing. How could
he wait that long?

He was walking past the tent on his way

to watch the procession arrive, when he had
an idea. The main entrance had a sign
across it saying 'Not open until three', but
just here, at the side, there was a flap that
wasn't done up properly. He took a quick
look round. Nobody about. He crawled in.

To Gary's great surprise, only a few
metres away, there was a small group of
people looking at pots of jam and bottles
of home-made wine. The judges hadn't

finished yet! In a panic, he slid under the nearest table.

Scuff dealt with Banger's careless knot by tugging. Then he leaped Miss Gale's garden wall, nosed open the back door, which had been left ajar, and was disappointed to find nothing edible in the kitchen. He trotted back to the deserted High Street and along

to the village hall. When he got to the Show tent he sat down and had a good scratch. Whatever those boys had done to his coat was beginning to make him itch. Then his long nose twitched with curiosity. There was a gap in the white wall in front of him, and a distant but promising smell of some kind of food . . . Scuff pushed his way in, tail wagging.

What luck! He was right by a table loaded with delicious flans, scones and cakes. In a flash, both huge forepaws were on the snowy white tablecloth and a complete sponge cake had disappeared down the ravenous throat of the Werewolf of Rockdown!

Chapter Six

The boys and Miss Gale were pounding up the High Street with aching sides and heaving chests. Miss Gale was handicapped by her long skirt, Eggy by his paint-can feet and Banger by the bandages slipping over his eyes. All of them were wondering what Clare Wilkins was doing, clinging on to the back of the lorry.

Clare was only there by the skin of her teeth. Her eyes were closed and her jaw clenched with the effort of holding on. Every bone in her body felt shaken to bits. Then the lorry slowed down as they went uphill and she opened her eyes.

'Oh! Stop!' she yelled, trying to attract the driver's attention. She turned to see if there were any passers-by who would help.

'Help! Help! Hel . . . aaaaaaargh!' Her
shout turned into a scream of fright. Only

a few metres away was a horrific freak, lurching towards her with outstretched hands dripping with blood. Behind this apparition was a sinister bandaged figure trailing clouds of white dust. Clare felt her arms and legs go limp with terror, the lorry gave a sudden lurch, and with a despairing wail she fell into the road, right into the path of the advancing ghouls.

'Ow!'

'Oooooh!'

'Oh my goodness!'

In the resulting tangle, Clare was relieved

to recognize the voices of Eggy, Banger and Miss Gale. She picked herself up. But when she put her right foot down a sudden pain shot up her leg. She limped a bit, hopped a bit, and then started to cry. The lorry, carrying the maypole head, disappeared round the bend – but that hardly mattered now, if she wasn't going to be able to dance!

The judging of the Fancy Dress was over. The Rockdown Majorettes were lined up on the green in their blue and gold uniforms and the village band were tuning up. The maypole dancers stood in an anxious group. Where was Miss Gale? She should be here to sort them out for the parade. And there were two people missing. Barry Winters had come out with mumps that very morning and there was no news at all of Clare Wilkins.

The Fancy Dress children shuffled into a line behind the float. On the float, amid a riot of paper flowers and swathes of curtain material, was Bonnie Dean on a low stool next to the very grown-up seventeen-year-old Linda Foster, who was seated on a gold-painted throne. The Rockdown Queen was giggling and waving, as friends and relatives stood round taking photographs. Bonnie could hardly raise a smile. This was awful. Even worse than she had thought.

Her mother was waving at her.

'Bonnie! I'm going down to the Show field to take some photographs of you arriving.' Mrs Dean turned to go and Bonnie gave a sigh of relief. She brought out her glasses from underneath a fold in her skirt. She might be pretending to be a princess for the afternoon, but there really was no good reason why a princess shouldn't wear glasses. She put them on as

the tractor pulling the float started up. As
they slowly began to move forwards behind
the band, Bonnie was able to see properly
again. They pulled away from the church
towards the sharp, narrow bend that led
into the High Street.

Just then a lorry came roaring round the
corner and with a squeal of brakes
scrunched to a halt only inches away from
the leader of the band. The music stopped
abruptly and there was a lot of shouting
between the bandsmen and the two men in
the cab of the lorry. The procession came
to a ragged stop. The street was so narrow

at this point that the lorry couldn't possibly get by.

'I'm not backing into the High Street,' shouted the lorry driver. 'You'll have to reverse to the green.'

'I'm not reversing this bloomin' great
thing!' the tractor driver yelled in return.
The truck started to edge forward, tooting

its horn. The band leaped on to the pavements. The tractor and the truck were now nose to nose.

Then Linda Foster did a very unqueenly thing. (But it was her great day, and she wasn't going to let it be spoilt.) She stood

up on the float and shook her bouquet at the lorry men.

'Oi! You! Get off out of it!' she bellowed.

'I'm not sitting here all day!' Bonnie was beginning to enjoy herself. Everyone was staring at Linda. Then all the heads turned as if they were watching a tennis match, because there was shouting from behind the lorry and pushing and shoving in the crowd. People jumped back in alarm as Frankenstein's Monster, the Mummy from the Tomb and a distraught Victorian lady waving a hat made their way to the front of the lorry.

'You've got the top of the maypole,' gasped Banger and Eggy together.

'Yer what?' The driver gazed at their extraordinary appearance in amazement. Miss Gale explained.

'You took some scrap from behind my house, only you took our maypole head as well — two metal plates with rings through them.'

'No. Didn't take nothing like that.' The driver's mate was sure.

'I can see it! I can see it!' called a voice from above. It was Bonnie. Standing on the float, she could see into the back of the lorry, and among the tangle of corrugated iron, rusty springs and rotting pushchairs, she had caught sight of the precious maypole head.

The next few moments were confused, as Miss Gale rushed off to the field to supervise the putting up of the maypole, and one of the Fête organizers persuaded the lorry driver to reverse.

While the parade was sorting itself out, Banger and Eggy hopped up on to the float and sat near Bonnie, their legs dangling over the side.

'We deserve a lift,' explained Banger. 'We've run for *miles*.'

'Shove up. You can give me a lift, too.' It was Clare, looking very miserable. Her pinafore was filthy and her knees scraped

raw. The boys hauled her on board.

'Honestly,' complained Queen Linda. 'This isn't the Rockdown bus you know.'

'Oh, let her,' pleaded Bonnie. 'She's hurt herself.' Linda looked doubtful, but as the float moved forward again she was distracted by having to wave regally at the bystanders lining the High Street.

'I can't dance,' sniffed Clare, 'and I won't get Miss Gale's prize. This was supposed to

be a Red Letter Day and it's turned out to be awful.'

'What about us?' complained Eggy. 'All the effort we put into making our costumes and buying make-up and stuff, and we go and miss the judging, chasing round after scrap lorries.'

'I suppose those Bridge House kids walked away with the Pairs prize,' said Banger, gloomily.

'They didn't!' announced Bonnie, triumphantly. 'The judge hardly looked at them. She gave first to the Barker twins. They've made a dragon out of apple packing trays and yoghurt pots and she said it was very original and it was nice that they'd done it all themselves. The Bridge House children didn't even come third!'

'I bet she would have liked ours,' sighed Eggy, regretfully.

'You look fantastic,' agreed Bonnie. 'Really revolting . . . all that blood and slime! By the way, what happened to Scuff?'

The float just happened to be passing Miss Gale's house. There was no sign whatsoever of the Werewolf of Rockdown.

Chapter Seven

It was agreed afterwards that Rockdown Primary's Red Letter Day hadn't turned out quite like anyone had expected. There were surprises from start to finish – and a lot of coincidences, or 'Big Ifs', as Eggy called them.

If Miss Gale had been her usual efficient self, the head of the maypole would not have gone missing. If Gary Wilkins had been able to wait until the Show tent opened to see if he had won anything, he would not have been on hand to prevent Scuff from eating all the food exhibits. If Bonnie had not been wearing her glasses, she would not have seen the maypole top, everyone might have believed the scrap metal men, and it would have been lost for ever. If Clare had not bravely jumped on to the lorry, she wouldn't have had a fall. If she hadn't hurt her ankle, and Barry Winters hadn't had mumps, Miss Gale would not have been short of two maypole dancers. If Miss Gale hadn't been short of dancers, she would not have had to ask Patrick East and Tom Morgan to help her out . . .

'But we haven't practised!' objected Eggy.

'You know Double Trace and Barber's Pole backwards. You've been doing them since you were in Mrs Padfield's class.'

'But just look at us!' urged Banger. 'There isn't time to go home and change and get all this gunge off.'

Miss Gale first looked at Eggy and shuddered. Then she turned her attention to Banger.

'Can't we just unwind you?' Banger

backed away.

'No fear! I've only got pants on
underneath!' Miss Gale sighed heavily and

then put on her 'I Have Made Up My Mind' face.

'Patrick — take off the stilts. Tom — try to uncover your face a bit. You'll just have to dance as you are. There isn't anyone else who knows those two dances. *Please*, boys.'

The Monster looked at the Mummy. The Mummy gave a nod. It was reluctantly agreed. Eggy and Banger to the rescue again.

The sun shone kindly on Rockdown Fête and Flower Show. It shone on the brightly coloured stalls around the arena, on Linda Foster's glittering crown and on the twinkling batons of the Majorettes as they marched round the ring. Rockdown Primary children were everywhere, among the Majorettes coming out of the arena and the dancers waiting to go in, pushing through the crowd in the Show tent or running from stall to stall with pocket money clutched in sticky hands.

Clare stood holding on to a whining, wriggling Scuff as the music began and the maypole dancers skipped into the ring. Scuff felt hard done by. That cake had been delicious. Why had that interfering boy stopped him from sampling the other goodies that had obviously been laid out specially for him?

'I know how you feel,' Clare consoled him. 'It's pretty miserable for me, too. It's a funny thing, though . . . even though I can't dance, I'm glad it didn't have to be cancelled.'

The first three dances looked as pretty as a picture. Spider's Web, Plait the Rope and Gypsy's Tent, danced by demure and solemn Victorian children. Not a single ribbon got tangled, no one went the wrong way and everyone kept perfect time.

The old-fashioned effect was a little spoiled in the last two dances. When the Monster and the Mummy joined the group, their partners for the Double Trace seemed reluctant to go near them.

'Ugh!' complained one girl. 'I'm not dancing with *him*!'

'I'm not holding hands,' declared the other. 'He's all slimy!'

'Don't be such babies,' hissed Miss Gale from the sidelines. 'Get on with it.' The girls looked at one another, pulled faces, and did as they were told.

The next and final dance turned into a comedy routine. As the dancers turned to unwind the pattern, the end of the Mummy's bandage began to work loose. Gradually and inevitably, Banger began to unravel. Bravely he struggled on, until the

girl behind him stepped on the trailing bandage. The unravelling speeded up. Banger clutched frantically at the remaining strips around his middle, while the rest drifted around the other dancers. By the end of the dance the maypole ribbons were unwound, but everyone's legs were tied up in strips of white cotton and Miss Gale had to rush around with a pair of scissors cutting them free.

There were more surprises. When the clapping had died down, Miss Gale announced, 'I would like to tell you about the winner of my annual prize. This is awarded to the dancer who has worked the hardest and made the most progress during the term. This year's winner, because of an unfortunate accident, couldn't dance today, but she is here, watching . . . Clare Wilkins.'

Clare could hardly believe it. She hadn't danced, but she had won the prize all the same! She limped forward, Scuff trotting at her side. Miss Gale was holding out a parcel with a big red ribbon round it. My lucky colour, thought Clare, happily. But Scuff had got there just in front of her. Thinking the parcel was being offered to him, he snatched the ribbon with his teeth and pulled.

Bonnie was still enjoying herself. It had been great fun watching Eggy and Banger in the maypole dancing, and now there was this tug-of-war contest with Scuff on one side and Miss Gale on the other. How very clever of Scuff to know that Miss Gale always gave a big box of chocolates as the prize!

Gary had missed his sister's moment of glory. He was positioned by the entrance to the Show tent, ready to pounce on every relative, friend or enemy who came in. He wanted to make sure that everyone knew that he, Gary Wilkins, had won three first prizes and that his miniature garden had

won the cup for the best children's exhibit
in the Show.

He had even won first prize in the open
cookery section for his sponge cake — but
no one would ever know that, except for

Eggy and Banger. Because it was to save
Banger from the wrath of the vicar's wife
that he had swapped his beautiful sponge
cake for the one wolfed by Scuff. While the
judges' backs were still turned, he had swept
off the crumbs, put the vicar's wife's label
by his own cake and removed the label that
said Gary Wilkins. Then quickly and quietly
he had dragged Scuff out of the tent and
away from further temptation. He looked
forward to telling his heroes how he had
covered up for Scuff, meanwhile . . . Aha!
There was Mr Fisher. He tugged at the
head's sleeve.

'Sir! Look over there. Can you see my
cup?' Mr Fisher went over to look and was
duly impressed. Gary glowed inside. This
was one in the eye for his know-it-all sister!

Two weeks later and the Fête still wasn't
over, as far as Rockdown Primary was
concerned. They were only just finishing

Mr Fisher's project. The wall behind the piano was covered in writing and pictures from all the three classes. Miss Gale's class had done a lovely big collage of the maypole dancing. There were mounted photographs of all the events, newspaper cuttings and prize cards, including three red ones with Gary's name on.

The photos had been sent in by various parents and Bonnie had arranged them with captions underneath so that they told the story of the whole day.

There was one with the float and the lorry nose to nose and Linda Foster waving her flowers with a scowl on her face. There was one of herself, pointing dramatically as she caught sight of the missing maypole top. There were ones of the Fancy Dress, the Majorettes and the maypole dancers, including Frankenstein's Monster and the Mummy from the Tomb. There was a super one of Scuff and Miss Gale struggling over

the dance prize, taken in close-up, and
another of Clare, holding a battered box of
chocolates over her head as if it were a
football trophy.

Scuff featured in another snap, in a head-
on confrontation with the Barker twins'

dragon. There was a good photograph from the newspaper of Gary, holding his miniature garden, and the final one was a dramatic action shot of Mr Fisher and some other men taking down the maypole at the end of the day. It was a pity that one or two of the dads had spent so much of the afternoon in the beer tent and that the pole had slipped and come down too quickly . . .

In Class One, Mr Fisher was writing very shakily, with his left hand, on the board

MY RED LETTER DAY – JULY 25TH

He turned round, adjusting the sling of his plastered right arm.

'Now, everybody . . .' The head raised his voice above the babble of noise. Class One had been impossible since the Fête. '*My Red Letter Day* is coming up quite soon,' he said firmly. The talking died down and Eggy and Banger shelved their plan for tying the Barker twins' plaits to the backs of their chairs. 'July the twenty-fifth,' persisted the head. 'Anyone like to guess why it's a Red Letter Day for me?'

'It's your birthday?' guessed Clare Wilkins, first as usual. Mr Fisher shook his head.

'You're going to have your plaster off?' suggested Bonnie Dean. Mr Fisher said no, unfortunately not that soon. The class were puzzled. They couldn't think of anything else exciting that could be happening to Mr Fisher.

'Give up?' inquired Mr Fisher, throwing his chalk up into the air and catching it. He turned back to the blackboard.

MY RED LETTER DAY – 25TH . . . IS . . . (Mr Fisher added) . . . THE FIRST DAY OF THE HOLIDAYS!

Class One cheered in wholehearted agreement. Next to the Rockdown Fête and Flower Show, it was the best thing that happened all year!